very best wishes
A C Clarke

Messages of change

Callender
2015

A C Clarke

Oversteps Books

First published in 2008 by   Oversteps Books
6 Halwell House
South Pool
Nr Kingsbridge
Devon
TQ7 2RX
UK

www.overstepsbooks.com

Oversteps Books acknowledges with thanks the financial
assistance of Arts Council England, South West

Printed in Great Britain by imprint digital, Devon

Acknowledgements

Some of these poems or versions of them have appeared in the following magazines and anthologies: 14, Envoi, Images of Women, The Interpreter's House, Markings, Mslexia, New Voices Press anthologies, The New Writer, Orbis, Poetry News, Poetry Nottingham, Poetry Scotland, Second Light, Textualities, Thin Bright Blade, Ver Poets' publications, Weyfarers, Wild, various other competition anthologies, Zed2O.

Empress Eugenie Visits Her Unfinished Tapestry At Farnborough won the 2005 Petra Kenney Award.

Listening for Orpheus won the 2007 Brownsbank International Poetry Competition.

The Builders was commended in the 2008 Poetry on the Lake competition.

I am indebted to Valerie Thornton for her invaluable advice on ordering and editing these poems.

To the memory of Joan Fry, distinctive poet, acute critic, wise and witty friend

For all the many people, family, friends, fellow poets, who have given me support and encouragement over the years

CONTENTS

MOONCHILD

'Moon!' you cry 'Moon! Moon!'
Ted Hughes, 'Full Moon and Little Frieda'

The Moon caught his eye – he ceased crying
immediately. And his eyes and the tears in them, how
they glittered in the moonlight!   S T Coleridge,
'Notebooks'

As if it had to be done.

To take the child out
from the warm house
into the cold evening.

To set them face to face,
the old pocked moon,
the eyes newly opened,

light pouring onto the upturned face
moon-blessing,
white baptism.

SIMEON'S PROPHECY

Yea, a sword shall pierce through thy own soul also
(Luke, Ch.2, v.35)

He did not need a prophet's eyes,
old Simeon, seeing that young mother.

So many mothers
had held their children out for God's approval
each thinking hers
love's perfect Word.

This was no different. Perhaps
the sun gleamed, breaking cover
as he signed blessings over
the eggshell skull,
its tender spot unclosed still,

the woman turned aside,
covered her face
looking inward a while -
no other omen.

Wise in old histories, he could read
stigmata in a mother's hands that bleed
the instant of quickening,
see through her wounded side
the heart's intricate channels lanced,
water and blood mingling.

THE DOLL
For my mother

Your father brought it home
a sailor's gift from the blue
your ebony doll
eye-whites startling as snow
lips redder than blood.

That wooden-hearted image
out of old tribes
spoke to you of darkness and heat
flies buzzing with fevers
the sorcerer's bone.

But you'd have none of it.
Sturdy and sensible as your t-strap sandals
you knew it would take sick
couldn't survive
our prim summers.

You gave it the full works
just in case:
a shoebox coffin
net veils for the mourners
a solemn procession.

Three foot under
with family for witness
you buried your fear,
sealed, tamped down
in good Kent clay.

Dealt with all doubts
the same way.

SEPIA PHOTOGRAPH

She glowers at the lens, resenting
her legs encased in frilly drawers
the party frock she wasn't allowed to dirty.

Her look homes into the future, the way
she looked death in the face
refusing pretence.

Her small sailor-suited brother
perches anxiously on the studio
rocking-horse. He doesn't foresee.

They grew apart. After she died
he sent a wreath of flowers
'To a wonderful sister'.

AT BYRON ROAD

This door opens into the memory
of my grandmother's house: the smells
of polished wood, roast meat and cooking cabbage
hovering in the hallway assume the shapes
that made her world certain. The walnut clock

tut-tuts on the mantelpiece where three
carved elephants march single file
above the hiss and spurt of a damp-coal fire
prisoned by its brass guard. On the table
the custard yellow plates with scalloped borders

display the Sunday teatime lurid pink
tinned salmon on a bed of fading lettuce
which must be eaten under the massed stare
of black-and-white sailors pinned to the walls,
gunbarrels behind them pointing seawards.

I'll leaf through back numbers of *Picture Post*,
while Grandad, a graduate, he says,
of the world's university, picks up
one of the two conches from the hearth,
presses against my ear the whole Pacific.

HARTLEY AND THE STARS

From an incident recounted in Coleridge's notebooks

When I am a man

I will get a ladder and climb
to the sky. With my clasp-knife
I'll dig each star from its skin
like eyes from a potato.

I'll thread them on
the spun hair of a comet,
for Anny Sealy
to wear round her moon-white throat.

When I am a man.

A SONNET FOR HOMEWORK

'Write a sonnet for homework,' Miss Orton said –
she was 'Miss' to us despite her stockbroker husband
(they each had a separate bed:
'It's more hygienic, girls'). Convent-trained
in obedience, we grappled Petrarchan, Shakespearean,
trochee, iamb, the five foot line,
permutation of couplet and quatrain –
managed it, more or less, except Geraldine,
whose poem 'Death in the Electric Chair'
('You're so morbid, girls') followed no set
pattern, didn't rhyme, let alone scan, was easily more
than fourteen lines, and yet
after all these years, in the mind's ear still crackles:
live, sparky, bursting out of its shackles.

COCKLE PICKERS

On a beach beside the Channel
fifty years back, a child is scrabbling sand
brown as fudge. The tide has left
its slew of lost belongings: crinkled kelp ribbons
still shiny-wet, black bladderwrack,
mermaids' purses, shards of cuttle-bone,
spiny urchin-cases, their tenants gone.

All this to her eyes is a marvel.
Stranger, more wonderful, the trails
of creatures burrowed under her very feet.
She spots her prize, the short, smooth track
of new-dived cockle. Her fingers poke,
excited by her father's praise, the thrill
of catch and eat. Out comes a tight-shut shell.

It's getting dark. She's not afraid.
The grown-ups have their torches. Round the bay
strings of light swing along the esplanades.
The tide is a refrain still yards away.
Here, bending to her task, she feels at home.
Her basket fills up, slowly.
Later, by lamplight, she will taste the sea.

Next day down at the tide's edge
she'll take the weight of waves on her thin chest
and shriek with half fear as the grown-ups watch.
She'll gasp and tumble and spit salt
laughing, unthinking. Years away
from those whose cries the wind drowns as it whips
seawater to their thighs, waists, shoulders, lips.

MEETING A STRANGER

This morning she dresses carefully
in secretary's black and white,
combs her hair to a shine.

Tucked among her vanities
she fingers the outline
of her passport to dreams.

She is going to meet a silken whisper
a briefcase full of surprises
a fairy godfather.

He is waiting for her at the terminus
propitiating his nerves with cigars.
His hand quivers as it touches hers.

This evening, glimpse of black and white
through briars, tufts of torn hair:
a face upturned, quenched stars.

THE WEE NED'S VALENTINE

Pale teenager on the bus
glugging Buckie, slams
the empties along the aisle, yells
into his mobile
'You'd better be there, babe.
I'll fucking cause CHAOS.'
Then, sotto voce,
'I love you.'

ODD COUPLE

Each day she's there for the pickings,
an apple core, a spat seed. Common as muck.

Sometimes he watches, sometimes scoops
this morsel of feather into his King Kong paw

holds her so light she balances easy
button eyes probing his own deep caves

with not a flicker, while his massive brow
frowns with tenderness.

Perhaps he feels her small hot heart
hammering through the softness of her breast

five times the speed of his, alas.
She perks in and out meanwhile

airy as he is grounded.
Her claws tickle like fleas

-- his mother's gentle fingers searching --
her chirrup opens his silence.

When she flies off, he sits for hours
stares at the open sky.

IN SOLITARY

Mornings are best,
the air's mouth rinsed of yesterday. If sun
walks in my patch of sky, it's almost cheerful.

Noon sits heavy on the eyelids. Waking,
I'm ringed by faces.
We bare teeth at each other.

Sometimes a small bird perches in my palm
or hops about pecking at melon seeds,
chirruping in an unknown dialect.

Evenings I sink into my folds of flesh
watch how the sullen day draws back
barred by steel clouds.
Around me jungle voices greet the dusk.
So close; so far away.

BELONGING

The garden air, still rain-heavy,
breathes cool after indoors. A gentleness there
and in the hooded light, as if it were
fading in an old photo, to the point
almost of being invisible. People are moving
slowly, talking in low voices.
Nothing to do with me. I raise a hand
to this honeysuckle flower, pearls still hanging
from soft lobes, bend to take in
watered sweetness – deeper, like damp skin
after bathing – feel how much at ease
it lives with itself, before I let it fall
back into place, my momentary touch
effaced already. Havering among
unhurried things, I am drawn back
into the framework of time and tension
the struts that brace us against each other
and as an urgency of words flows over
the spaces between selves, I watch – we watch –
moths lured too close to our hot dazzle
flare for an instant, fizzle out.

LIZARD DUET
(a poem for two alternating voices, herpetologist and lizard)

Lacerta Vivipara
of the sub-order Lactilia
                    I know to exactness
                    when the sun-bathed
                    stone is warm enough
                    for my loaded belly, when
                    each flagging cell in my cold body
commonly found in scrub, in heathland
in all parts of this island.
                    is volted again.
                    When the kicking life inside me
                    crescendos
I have netted, measured, weighed
counted toes, enumerated scales
                    when the shadows of beak and wing
                    cross my daylight
have been known to use scalpels.
                    I know what to do
I know what this is.

This is: a picture in my textbook
                    I am scale. I am skinny-bone. I
                    am eyes.
                    Sponge for sunlight, throwaway
                    tail.
one of three British lacertids
                    I am younglings seething like worms.
grey-olive to brown in colour, with variants
                    I am warmth, chill, pain, release -
                    the moment.
distinguished from snake by movable eyelids.

I do not think. I am.
>   *Brain the size of a peanut*
Being takes all I have
>   *three half-digested flies*
>   *in the simple gut.*
is all I can.

OVERHEARD

I've heard you once only.
Your voice, liquid and trilling,
half-matched poetic flattery.
I remember thinking
a thrush or blackbird not far off the mark
though neither's found your fame, bulbul
of Persian gardens, muse
of dying poets, who sings in the dark,
voice of silenced Philomel –
so the story goes –

telling over and over her human wrong.
You're a plain bird,
small. Would we notice your song
in daylight, when every tree in the wood
broadcasts? You've had to bear
a weight of meaning –
how could we resist
turning you into metaphor?
Our thoughts take wing
so easily, seldom return to roost,

as you must, bound to the humdrum
of food, rest, mate.
We want you in a poem
not out looking for flies. Too late
to bring you back to nature
ancient icon.
You join the turtle dove,
the rose, your eastern lover,
the whole well-thumbed lexicon
of the language of love.

But when I heard you, nightingale,
in a nameless city square
you were yourself. You couldn't tell
who might be listening; didn't care.
I wasn't moved to words.
How could I better
all that's been written?
You were a bird among other birds
just happening to be there.
I just happened to listen.

OBSERVED

In the Jardin Des Plantes the panther
(the hollow in its flank a sculptor's nightmare)

narrows eyes as green as malachite;
the poet set to cage it in a sonnet

notes dutifully the power, the grace
turning and turning in its narrowed space

under that electric fur the dart
of nerves, the hammering heart –

he knows. The panther never stops its circle
around the still point – scribble, scribble –

then just at one half-turn pauses to stare
straight through the eyes of metaphor.

FEVER HOSPITAL, CORROUR

These blocks are grey, like prison drabs,
but air is running freely through
the cordon sanitaire they set here
a thousand feet above the valley floor
clear of the phlegms coughed up by bogs

out of reach except by ponies
that jolted plague-carts up the path
bringing sour bodies haloed in carbolic.
Imagine how it was: you'd wake
from quinined sleep to the stern smiles

of nurses, hands expert in stripsearch,
to days of simmer under red blankets
that smelled of sick: long days
with nothing to do but be ill
until the verandah, the propped pillows –

even with snow floating in –
where you'd watch high clouds
up and away over a chain of hills
your weak breath shouted down by burns,
by frogs in meltpools stashed with spawn

the bed next yours empty that morning
the parents' parcel returned to sender
nurses on thermometer duty
and you lying there, wrists thin as birdbone
listening to all that life.

TOMOGRAPHY OF AN EMBRYO

A coil of seagreen spinal nerves
and grey veined slabs
like uncooked soft roe.

Where are your eyes?
Could that small sponge
dissolving into slush become your brain?

Blue for your spinal cord, we're told
'and other tissue': you're tangled in
too many folds to unravel.

You could be anything watery
– squid, nautilus, seahorse –
but for that one vital organ,

already set to tap its chamber music
right in the centre, the shape
and shade of a ripe strawberry:

we have to take their word
for what you are – here at least
they've stained you the colour of life.

ENTERING THE MUMMY

He's knocking at your ribs. Your heart
hasn't been bottled. Soon he'll have it out
for a good look. In the cave of your bones
there's pickings to be had.

Even your skin tells tales. He'll chip off flakes
like a geologist. For there you lie
sex naked as death
all your protections looted.

You've been prepared
against gang-rape by worm and spider.
No-one foresaw this bugger but
he's not the first in.

Remember while you waited for death
the whispers in the room you couldn't speak to,
a king no longer in charge. Already
they were whetting knives for your belly.

If only the blades that slice into your secrets
were tender as fingers
stretching to touch
the vanishing hem of your spirit.

FLINTSHAPER

Under his apefingers stone
chipped flake by patient flake
curves obedient to the hand's hollow.
Drawing his thumb across the cutting edge
he knows the fitness of the thing,
its weight and certainty, how it tears
raw hide, drills out a demonic skullbone.
He will warm his kin with its sparks.

Growing under his fingers,
flake by patient flake,
cold perfection of steel
sheathed in the breastbone
precision of the bomb hatch
sliding back softly.
He turns the flint in his hand,
over and over.

FORTUNES OF WAR

He lies, an arm outflung, as if at rest,
not sleeping. By a trick of light the eyes
look at you, questioning. A cloud of flies
buzzes his puffed out belly. He is dressed
as if for leisure, basking in the sun
which warms his swelling limbs. The country shirt
bare at the throat is stained with more than dirt.
His hand lies open, innocent of a gun,
two fingers hacked off – enemies' mockery.
Skin flakes from his sunk cheeks – he will rot here.
'Fortunes of war,' his wry grin seems to say,
'I might have done the same – don't back away.
Although I stink, I'm quiet company.
It's not the dead the living need to fear.'

AMPUTEE
Photograph in an exhibition

Poised as a Benin bronze, her head's proud angle
the first thing that I notice, next
the calm of her hands. She seems to cup sunlight
between folded palms. As I come close
her gaze travels through me. I can't read it.

When I become aware her flowered frock
hides neither her slender right leg nor
its clumsy wooden mockery on the left
I don't know what I feel. Is it shock?
Distaste she's let herself be made a peepshow?

No. Curiously she seems complete
seated in massive repose
like an Egyptian deity. One who knows
in every fibre human cruelty,
rough human kindness. Meets both with grace.

GARDEN NEAR AMIENS

In this sheltered corner of Picardy
flowers are blooming every which way –
full-blown roses, mauve swags of the butterfly tree,

gold poppies, zinnia in shades of red
not one of which is remotely the colour of blood.
This garden is heaving with growth, it's buried

the new shed waist-deep, it's shaded over
an older shed with an awning of creeper,
it's pushing up through stem, leaf, stamen, flower.

There's a posse of bees raiding
these open stores of nectar, the air humming.
Everyone else at rest, drinking

under red and white parasols
stuck jauntily at outside tables.
Rich soil, this must be. Generous.

And on a day like this, when sky
is still as a pond and petals noiselessly
widen, you wonder how anything can die.

HELLISH NELL

marked out from the first
by her inconvenient habit of flipping a shutter
letting light in from beyond
what was decent

climbed tomboy heights
wouldn't play ball
fritter with dolls

suddenly blurting out something
you'd rather not hear

scandalized Callander
parting her thighs
for a child that popped out
the wrong side of the tartan

learned to give birth
to the dead,

one fine evening
(spirit-tranced above a chemist's in Portsmouth)
skewered with searchlights
by possessing policemen
was charged with conjuring -

too late to stop
the thousand souls downed by torpedo
floating gauzily
out of her ice-cold mouth.

*The childhood nickname of the clairvoyant Helen Duncan, the last
person tried for witchcraft in Britain, arrested allegedly because she
revealed in a seance that a British ship had been sunk by German
torpedoes, months before the Government released this information.*

WHITE LACE TABLECLOTH

kept for weddings,
christenings,
abandoned in this ditch
wrapping a small,
disturbing shape
and sealed with sticky tape
like a gift:
which would, unwrapped,
bring tears
if after endless wars
there were tears left.

EMPRESS EUGENIE REVISITS HER UNFINISHED TAPESTRY AT FARNBOROUGH

Her satin-slippered feet skim the oak treads
of the main house, out of bounds to the boarders.
A single light burns dully in the hallway
which used to light her ivory-powdered skin
with the kind glow of candelabra.

She pauses on the landing under the huge
picture in which, all silks and ermine,
she plays the Empress. There is no-one
waiting to admire her bouffant skirts
afloat on the grand, still handsome, staircase.

She listens. She can hear the old house wheezing
down ageing passageways, once velvet-thick
to step into, like moss. Hardshod now
with brown harsh-smelling lino slathered over
by a perfunctory mop, but holding still

for her the after-image of his dear
eau de cologne. She breathes his manliness
and sees his silver-backed pure bristle brushes
laid out in their obedient ranks
on his dressing-table, feels again

the sleekness of his oiled moustache
against her upper lip. She knows the way
in the dark, through the heavy door
along the gallery. Gathering her skirts
she hurries as she once would not have done.

Here it is, here. Just within her reach,
the yards of half-worked cloth she started on
to keep her fingers from blame, and let her thoughts
wander to where he rode or lounged
or did whatever men did in their world

those boudoir afternoons when the sun seemed
to draw a heavy odour from the swags
of drapery and send the air to sleep
as she stitched on, listening to a lady
read the latest romance, or plink

a harp's stretched strings. She put their life
into this work. She leans across
the railing that protects it, in her hand
a crewel needle she threaded herself
from a skein of coloured silk.

Quick now, before night starts to thin.
What will it be this time, cross-stitch,
rococo, Florentine? She slips it in.
A hundred stitches – one for every year
and nowhere near the end. She's making it last.

MEDITATION AT FASLANE

You'll catch your death my mother used to say.
Death isn't so easy. Can't be trapped
in coils of damp hair or down the neck
of a flimsy blouse. As I stand stamping my feet
outside the razor-wire three fences deep
I think about death,
how we wrap up warm against it.
How babies have died
from too many blankets.

And I think about my mother,
doing what mothers
are meant to – she'd learned it from hers.
If she saw me standing here 'You must be frozen!'
she'd cry and chatter on
of Grandad and the Navy, VE Day –
everyone dancing and kissing absolute strangers –
of war and rationing and black-out curtains
and how 'they' know what they're doing.

FRAGMENT

Yellow glaze on a chip of baked clay
cries out among this broken crockery
beached by the river's rise and fall.

A find?

'Victorian tile', he says, scarcely giving a glance.
I toss back a bit of kitchen or public urinal.
Which mattered once.

SHADES

Black: trees upright as sentinels,
a railway track that ends
at a long, low shed.
White: snow's blanket denial.

Grey: naked bodies in a queue,
hard soap, concrete floors, ash;
in these pictures the uniform
of sky, however blue.

LABORARE EST ORARE

God's work they tell him, though he'll not take chances
(crossed fingers, harespaw slipped behind a wall).
Days off Purgatory if he believes them
for stooping under a sack of rubble.

On a good day he might unbend
from some bone-aching task to see a blue
pure as the Madonna's cloak stretch miles
above his head - the panoply of saints

he's taught to praise surely at ease behind
that infinite screen, loudhailing the Deity
in Latin canticles from azure thrones.
He can hear, almost. Most days he knows

only the itch of lice under his jerkin,
the knot of pain across his shoulders.
His belly grumbles on weak beer and onions.
Buboes or bloody flux, it won't be long:

his mate's a snapped spine underneath the spire
that rockets masonry prayers to heaven,
his wife's a sacrifice to marriage vows,
a one-day daughter.

Adam's curse they tell him when he lolls
in the back pews while the Sunday rant
pelts him with stones and sweetmeats turn by turn.
If heaven's not what it's hyped he's been done.

THE BUILDERS

You'll see them in expensive manuscripts
swarming up scaffolding, trowel in hand
spreading mortar across a row of bricks,
carving ornate moulding, mixing lime and sand,
their hose and tunics spotless pastel. Grand
tiers of icing-white confectionery
rise round them, sugar dreams in masonry.

These artisans will climb into the sky
with the assurance of pantomime Jack
though nothing visible secures the high
ladders, and each encumbered back
suggests humped spines. No-one is ever slack
under the perpetual sun. No lunch breaks,
swigging bottles, idle joshing, piss-takes.

This is the master version, no question.
I'd like to think that love as well as sweat
went into the real thing too: attention
to finicking a belltower parapet
no-one would see close up, patience to fret
vaulting to lacework. They'd tell their sons for sure
'See, I was part of this – not the seigneur

flaunting his silks there in the gentry's pew.
all *he* did was moan how slow we were.
A dozen men were crippled, a good few
died: but wives and widows got no silver.
It's a fine church' – then single out a pillar
they'd tagged, or where they'd smuggled a lewd scene
under the deacon's choirseat back of the roodscreen

in the guise of a moral, to show who was really
in charge. Let's celebrate these nameless ones,
every calloused knuckle: their garlicky
laughter, ale-mugs, messes of tripe and onions,
their profane oaths, their smut. They'd conjure visions
out of stubborn stuff: saint, Virgin, hell-mouth yawning,
as soon as boast the girl they'd laid that morning.

SAMUEL DOW
After whom four pubs in Glasgow are named

Who was Samuel Dow?
Did he brew fine ales?
Somehow I can't see it.

I picture him in frock-coat and stiff wing-collar
beetling his brow
over the Times or the Scotsman
in a litter of toastcrumbs, his tea
cooling beside him in a porcelain cup

or taking the bow
at a municipal dinner after giving
a two hour speech on the profits of boilermaking
in which he told three heavily laboured jokes
and mopped his brow
repeatedly.
                    Samuel Dow.
I bet he didn't allow
even his wife to call him 'Sammy'.

I see him seven years old, rebuking his nurse
for being over-familiar
shaking hands with his mother
before retiring to sleep
with a book of maxims by his bed.

At thirty taking his vows
in a stentorian voice
while his bride, cowed
under her tonnage of diamonds
just whispers
'I do', not daring
to contradict.

Samuel Dow. The weight
of iron bridges
massive stanchions
quadruple chins
is in those syllables.

Where is he now?
And his fob and chain
his galoshes, his stovepipe hat
his cigar?

SIMON LEE'S VERSION
Alas! The gratitude of man/Hath oftener left me mourning
(William Wordsworth, 'Simon Lee The Old Huntsman')

A's out diggin' me garden, see, an' this falla'
(furriner, see, though 'e's leeved up yonder
these two year) cum up. Tall chap, bony.
Gennelman an'all. Weel, no' the likes o' me
any road. We sin him up yonder, takkin' a turn
roun' the garden, bumblin' away in a girt voice
fit ter frighten the crows. Dick sez ter me, 'e sez
'Yon's a poet.' 'Poet?', sez A, 'de'il A ken aboo' tha'.

Well, 'e cum up, see, as A's diggin'
this girt owld root. Reet bastard ov a root it were.
A'd let loup a few choice words, A kin tell ye.
An' 'e stan's there, the girt lummock. Stan's there
like 'e wuz growin' roots 'issell. An' A'm wheltin' this root
wi' me mattock, fit ter bust. An' then 'e sez
(in a reet fancy voice) 'You're overtaxed,
Simon. Give me your tool.' Wha' the fook – 'Gie me yer *tool*?'

Oh! The mattock! Reet! Weel, A wadden' say nae tae an offer
so A gies it 'im an' 'e splits tha' danged root in 'awf,
clean in 'awf, jis' like that, smiles ter 'issell
smug, like. 'Oh thank ye kindly sir' sez A
in me speakin' ter the gentry voice. 'thank ye kindly'.
But 'e's awa' at 'is bumblin' a'ready, tha' pleased wi' 'issell,
an A's fit ter bust agin: no' alang o' the root
(A's reet glad it's chopped) – alang ov *'im*.

ROPEMASTER

He's done this before, you can tell
as he hauls in the thin snake of a rope
tied to one end of the hawser, the big boat
prancing away from the dock, all
five thousand tons of her seemingly held
by this one man, whose steady pull

quiets her, as if schooling a restive mare.
All that's different is me watching
to catch the moment – quicker than thinking –
when he drops the hawser's looped end over
a bollard, moves away
coiling the free rope, unaware

he's looked at, focussed as a dancer
deep in the dance, each step so often taken
his limbs move of their own volition
through their routine, poised above the harbour
on a narrow steel walkway. He doesn't pause
to steady himself, consider

dangers, walks the length of the tethered boat,
to catch the aft rope, while the dock crew push
the heavy gangway up to a crush
at the opening doors. The fidget
of passengers impatient for off
won't make him change his pace. Without

a stumble or a break in rhythm
he takes his chosen time. And yet
I sense alertness in his shoulders, the set
of his head – master of equilibrium,
alive to the moment – in his left hand coiling,
the long, brown snake that trails behind him.

ARTIST ON THE METRO

On the blank canvas of her skin
she sketches in
an eyebrow. The train

rocks on its rails. Her hand
stipples a blue lid, blends
daubs of bright colour, finds

a contour of bone,
highlights. Goes on
tinkering with its own creation.

Her stop approaches.
She lightly touches
her cheek, tucks her brushes

back in her make-up repertoire.
Steps, face on, into the future.

CHANGING

Lingerie counters are his ivory portal.
The slur of silk between finger and thumb
(against nipples, under crotch)
the supernumerary lace
tracing a bra-cup, frilling a knickerleg.
No mere arousal
this is the real thing
racks of slips, basques, camisoles
peachy as skin which doesn't need shaving.

Back home he enters softness
the give of pliant textures.
His skirts rustle.
Forget the knife and needle. For these minutes
he's into Woman, as dreamed.
He smoothes the creases in her slippery skin
tenderly: finds it fit.

ODE TO A DANDELION

Startling, your perfect egg-yolk yellow –
tripled in size would burst in our faces
with Van Gogh exuberance. This time of year
each of your florets overlaps its fellow
so neat we can't imagine your grubby droop
on August wasteland among plastic bottles,
rusting car-parts.
                Dandy lion indeed,
perking out of your ring of jagged leaves,
dapper, defiant, no garden namby-pamby,
all parts serviceable from bitter taproot
to the nectar-brimming petals bees go down on.

Airhead you may be, blowing
thistledown kisses into a taking wind –
your roots go deep,
fork into awkward crevices,
dig in for the duration. Dents de lion
snapping in salad, pissenlit decocted
in a phial of herbals, your white sap stickies fingers
to a nicotine stain, dark leaves
make no concessions to sweetness.

Your head's so often whipped from its stem –
you never say die.
come Armageddon, you'll rise again
in full glory to greet your sister sun.

MOTHER ELDER

I should have known you were a woman,
an old one. Nothing less would explain
your crotchets, serial untidiness,
how you get your fingers round everything.

You like old ground well broken up with rubble,
to live close to the door.
Warty and grey, you'd never take
to terraces on Tuscan hills. Not safe
to sleep under your cat-stink leaves
but anyone awake and standing
under your solstice shade at midnight
will see the world which rides beside us.

You'd pinch the child to goblin-bruises
that slept in your cradle. Strong as poison
your roots hold tight to your patch;
your berries puncture purple, like ticks.
You grow best where blood's spilt.

In summer you proffer gypsy flowers.
I'll not break the smallest spray.
Each time I pass you watch me, arms akimbo.

ELIPHIBIAN

What if the small black dot in the heart of the glop –
which even on tadpole terms seems unlikely to prosper
left out high and all but dry on the hillside
like a troubling child – were to bud in all directions:
the bulbous head blossoming two ears
lavish as palm-heads, the tail springing a tassel,
the folds at the edge of the mouth thrusting out tushes
the snout uncurling a trunk thick as liana

and as the bulk of the thing heaved to its feet
stepping out of discarded frills of jelly
it let loose out of that pink-tipped, pliant bassoon
triumphant blasts as its great feet quivered the grass.

Suppose it twice the size of anything seen
in our diminished days, as if the bones
of a mastodon uncovered on a beach
by the wash of tides were to take new flesh, its hide
smooth as butter, green and glistening as olives ...

What if this new-spawned wonder, scattering sheep,
thudded down to the small white tourist town
turning all heads from tea-towels printed with
doggerel,
tartan teapots, pottery seals –
the nemesis that all had been vaguely expecting
there in the carpark stuffing shrubs into its maw
before it waddled off to give the loch
its newest monster, capsized the small boats
tethered alongside the pier. Cameras clicking:

no-one knowing in the slightest what else to do.

LESSON

Stones? We take a stick to poke the water:
as if a weak electric current jerked it
a forelimb twitches, then becomes inert.

Tuned to the tempo of a tree
unfolding spring buds leisurely
to wood-doves which repeat again, again
coo, coo, coroo from garlic-scented woods
these two will take all day and never stir
from the unflurried pool where she'll lay down
in their weed cradles slender skeins of spawn.

O patient rhythms of amphibian lovers,
beyond the swift hot heartbeats of two-legged creatures,
the brain's unconscionable chatter –
ecstatic tedium! Consider toads.

ASSEMBLY OF BIRDS

Ardrossan and above the chinking masts
of the weekend sailboats, against a light
already dimmer-switched, before the moon
turns on full power, black flecks
like giant ash-flakes from some conflagration
too huge to think are tossed around the sky –

there is a pattern but not ours, the same
unvoiced consent as in a flock of pigeons
suddenly rising and wheeling and settling
on a rooftop, then off, veering widdershins back
and then the whole manoeuvre over again,
seemingly just for the hell

for we haven't a clue any more than we know
what the geese in the topfield near the road to Rothesay
parley about in their urgent patois
hundreds milling around as if in waiting
for some long-heralded event: for sure
it's not about us. We're unnoticed

just like the time we sat watching the constant
flicker and dart of pinkbreast chaffinches,
seizing their tiny beakfuls of nut and seed
speeding home to their nests as if they would never
forage again – then back in a couple of minutes.
An intricate ballet choreographed on the wing.

Parallel lives at the edge of attention
which every so often startle us out of our doze:
be it the laughter of townbred gulls
still harsh with the rasp of the sea, a swan in sail
or migrant swallows arranging themselves
in perfect chords on a stave of telegraph wires.

ODE TO NOT A NIGHTINGALE

Not you little brown bird with the huge voice –
you've had your turn.
In Berkeley Square today you'd hear
guffaws. This is for *you*
corvine survivalist
on everybody's blacklist
handsome in black and white tuxedo, tails –
you earn full marks for chutzpah.

Streetwise, you stab the chick in the egg
possess a nest through swagger.
No picky eater
you swallow leatherjackets whole
steal birdseed
from under the beaks of bluetits.
You'll tear the guts from binbags
soon as gralloch roadkill.

Bully boy you don't give a damn
head cocked, bright eye,
effing and blinding lovers.
You're the city made feather
in all its buzz and horror
the gangleader, the hoodie
with his stashed blade.

Don't mess with me you cackle
you with the notebook there
*don't shut **me** up*
in one of your shit poems.

LISTENING FOR ORPHEUS

I shall not hear him in houses, the man who sang
so trees, suspending the sea-sigh of their branches,
would have lifted their roots and danced
if they could, as the deer did, the cattle did
because his music slid into their veins, like
the clew through the labyrinth, disarming
the heavy-headed monster at the heart, and they found
in their little twinkling hooves a gaiety
they had not suspected, a lightness that had not been theirs
since the pastures of their youth

and those that had horns lowered them as an armed man
might lower his weapon: this music had taken away
the drive to prove and to thrust and to do down.

Need I go down into darkness like the one he searched for
so long, is it deep in the veined earth
he would find me, a single unmined seam of gold
caught in a candleglitter instant flashing
above my veiled head, as I walk towards him
in the float and wisp of my disembodied self
my long pale fingers yearning towards fitful
light? Not there -

Shall I hear him by the sea, the endless
heartbeat of water pulsing my ear
with an insistence larger than any
human requirement? No –

If I will hear him, if he will venture
even the whispered call of a single lutestring,
if he will overlook my imperfect pitch
I must find him where the crossroads meet

in the middle of a dank wood on a still morning
when rain is falling in straight lines, mist
distilling out of fungal earth, when birds
are saying nothing and all colourful winged insects
have yielded to the kingdom of snails that write
over fallen leaves the glistening news of their travel.

There, there if anywhere, if I go alone
if I stand very quiet, very attentive
quite empty of thought, impulse, desire
I might hear, as if from across
infinite distance, the faint far
melody that will unmake me
for ever, loose me into that same unthinking
dance that holds the universe together
god knows how.

ICE HOTEL

Palegreen as Glacier mints but far from brittle
these blocks would freeze your tongue, the merest lick
enough to burn and stick. What pillars, architraves
they shape, thick as cathedral stone,
letting light through dimly, like bottleglass,
all ghost-glimmer. Strong as an eggshell

the roof, a tonne of snow would quilt its curve
in deeper white, the fall no weightier
than feathers fluttering through the dreams
of guests zipped in cocoons, their breath
small spurts of steam in not quite zero cold,
hands dormouse-curled inside the wadding.

Come summer, and the polished corridors
are water. Not a hint. You might be standing
in that green circle where an Irishman
woke stuttering with whisky breath
his hands groping for remembered walls,
the cold fire of enchantment.

BLIND SPRING

The hedge flips water on my fingers:
I smell not rain
but loosening frost.
Fathoms of air
above me shift and part.

Heaviness lifts; the sun
stoops to caress my cheek,
timid and welcome
like the breeze

which blows into my nostrils
gentle as a horse-whisperer
messages of change.
Things are afoot
in the deep earth.

Worms sense it
and the first bee,
whose buzzing stumbles
among awakening odours.

Birds break out
of their long silence.
The seeds I pushed in months ago,
gritty as saltgrains between
finger and thumb,

will be hatched
their tendrils groping
through rucks of leaf-rot,
towards felt light.

Other books published by Oversteps

Anthologies: Company of Poets and Company of Four

David Grubb: An Alphabet of Light

Giles Goodland: Littoral

Alex Smith: Keyserling

Will Daunt: Running out of England

Patricia Bishop: Saving Dragons & Time's Doppelgänger

Christopher Cook: For and Against Nature

Jan Farquarson: No dammed tears

Charles Hadfield: The nothing we sink or swim in

Mandy Pannett: Bee Purple & Frost Hollow

Doris Hulme: Planted wth stones

James Cole: From the Blue

Helen Kitson: Tesserae

Bill Headdon: Picardy.com

Avril Bruten: In the lost & found columns

Ross Cogan: Stalin's desk

Ann Kelley: Because we have reached that place

Marianne Larsen: A Common Language

Anne Lewis-Smith: Every seventh wave

Mary Maher: green darlings

Susan Taylor: The suspension of the moon

Simon Williams: Quirks

Genista Lewis: Cat's Cradle

Alwyn Marriage: Touching Earth

Miriam Darlington: Windfall

Anne Born & Glen Phillips: Singing Granites

www.overstepsbooks.com